HUMANITIES

Julian Farmer

HUMANITIES

FAND MUSIC PRESS

First published in Great Britain 2014

Fand Music Press
Glenelg
10 Avon Close
Petersfield GU31 4LG

Copyright © Julian Farmer 2014

ISBN 978-0-9535125-8-4

Printed by
Meon Valley Printers, Swanmore, Hampshire 01489 895460

古之所谓"曲则全"者，岂虚言哉？
诚全而归之。

Laozi

ISLAND

There's a bridge over to this island,
on the pond, in the park –
the gardens laid out in
early twentieth century *chinoiserie*.

Sometimes, people sail toy boats here,
and, when the sun comes out, I eat
ice creams, sitting on the boulders
in this simple rock-garden.

My thoughts, here, are tranquil,
isolated, even inward-looking
but the view is not of the locality,
being global, panoramic, strange...

Many years ago, I read Plato,
right here, Camus and Sartre
and nothing seemed indivisible
to my youthful mind.

Only in this place, I sense the pull
of a golden thread, which comes
down to greet me – homespun
inklings of those younger days...

Here, I'm in two states of being,
all at once, because
there's a bridge over to this island,
my place of solitude.

VILLAGE

The world-village is my home,
and yet I never fly.
I hear the songs of maidens
grinding seeds in the quern
or the basket-weaver's complaint.

Poetry, you're a wealthy friend;
your house stands over the stream.
Many a shadow, many a gleam
of purpose answers your door
and swallows flit from your roof.

If there was silence in my heart,
I'd keep it forevermore,
but the 'pip' of the sparrow,
the anguish of war, and
the labourer's sigh never cease.

Death, you're hardly a friend,
and yet I know you so well.
You never speak, until it's too late,
your guarded look is so cold,
and your mouth reeks of ignorance…

But the hand of youth works the wheel,
digs, where digging is seen,
and covers its love
with a modest rebuke,
while the world sleeps endlessly on.

EN LOCATIF

The word is in the locative,
and here it has a temporal force.
The momentous day suddenly arrives.
Four gods disguise themselves as Nala.
But Damayanti prays for help,
sees her man, and is his bride.

A dense blue sky glowers over
Andhra Pradesh and Madhya Pradesh.
The whole of India squirms below:
dung fires, beggars, rickshaw-drivers,
spices frying in the pot, broken sewers –
life and danger everywhere.

Small, transistor radios squeak
with warbling, westernised, Indian pop.
The heat is like a sleeping drug.
But I am neither there, nor here,
in temperate England, for I'm in
my own locative, with my true love.

THE WAR

They are all dead now, Fletcher,
the Engineer, Jock and Taff. Yes,
they are all dead, the ones,
that made for La Bassée,
     and caught the fire.

The squalor and the dread of it,
the mud, machine-gun storms,
and the hatred, that will kill
eight million men,
     have finished them.

The gas – the dead, the dead – drowning
in lifelessness – and the show they made
in Mametz Wood, are how
we remember them, our people cast
     into war, like sand.

And some, that did not die, became
family men, rode out the years
between the living and the dead,
and yet remembered them – the Engineer,
     Jock and Taff.

These swam at Hove, picnicked
in Hyde Park, and talked
at parties near The Strand, but these,
too, are all dead now – Fletcher, the Engineer,
     Jock and Taff.

THE SURREY HILLS

They say the woods can hear your thoughts,
above Holmbury, or among
that blanket of green between Friday Street,
Coldharbour, Westcott and Leith Hill...

Their bent boughs murmur – whispering,
like old ladies, gossiping in church,
undermining the sensible and brave
intentions of the meek.

But the meek endure forever.
The mist of their energies
thick among the trees, they drift
from happiness to furthest sky.

Do not leave your work undone,
or take an hour for granted.
The seasons change. The woods will find
the lies within your heart.

THE FIRST FALL OF SNOW

My sky spills ice. The crystal snow
roams downward, chilling this
suburban scene. An artist
decorating sight, it paints
and whitens both the hedge
                    and path.

The greensward, buried in the race
to populate the earth with grains
of frozen water, is the spot,
the pedestal, from which I see
back towards the snows
                    of youth.

My love, as now, was for a world
unrepentant, and unhurt,
where certainty felt no restraint,
a flood of words, of touch, of breath,
like snowflakes falling on
                    my hair.

And here is danger, here I dare
to cross the ice of arrogance,
of unventured, and unspoilt
chances in my search for love,
which carries on, despite defeat
                    and loss.

But here, I see a perfect sight,
the world composed of harmony,
the memory of past success, adventures
only half relived – and particles
of snowy dust – each a microscopic
                    jewel.

ANGELA

It was deathly, finding myself inside
a psychiatric hospital again,
although the first time's the worst,
when you can't yet believe
your liberty's been robbed...

"It'll be like the wrath of God,
when Sadiq finds that we've
been smoking in here!" I said to her.
"The wrath of God's nothing
compared to my father's wrath!"

she sneered sourly. Her face
looked like a giant question-mark
that asked and asked, but never found an answer.
She smoked, sold trinkets round the hospital,
which her sister had brought in for her.

"It's *his* voice I hear *all* the time,
shouting at me, just telling me what,
and he's been dead fifteen years. He'll never
go away..." She scratched her bandaged wrist.
I liked her. She was pretty.

NIGHT ANGEL

Such strange dreams, such strange
disembodiments of blighted worlds
populate my sleeping hours,
as the sun begins its climb to dawn.

Maybe I escaped Baghdad,
or roamed London, in bare feet, or played
at school again with faces seen
through decades of forgetfulness?

But I still know this angel
of night-tremors, and bleak surprises,
brings with her bold enlightenments
to my ever thankful mind.

WONDERING

I stare into infinity
every hour of the day.
You may think that my self-
awareness is a prop,
a weakness, an impediment
to energy and life.
But I see beyond the grey
sky and breaking dawn,
beyond my disillusionment,
my dry, though burning, heart.

And there I see the words
woven by the gods,
on dewy grasses, sunken leas
and memories of past
misdemeanours, casual jokes,
of languid books and loves.
And there, in that infinity,
I live a double life.
It gives answer to my grief
and redefines my sight.

AN OLD MAN'S THOUGHTS

All the things I remember in dreams
are the sights of a world
long forgotten…

All the things I remember awake
are stories that no one
wishes to hear…

All the things I remember in war
are facts that are far too
sad to recall…

All the things I remember in love
are you, my sweetheart,
my gentle one…

DER LEIERMANN

The Leiermann plays in the snow,
his hurdy-gurdy violin-like, only
he turns a handle and plays on and on.

My father liked Franz Schubert's take.
The portrayal of dejection thrilled us both,
as he neared the end: secondaries and death.

We'd keep company with the Leiermann,
perhaps sing a little, and beg for bread,
my life impoverished, his success.

Over and over, we played that track.
I bought a score for tenpence, and we learnt
the casual ripple of the notes.

At his funeral, I had to read
the lesson, being released from care
for five hours, but did not flinch

before the crowd, and remarked
that he wouldn't have wanted John.
"Is there something from Saint Paul?" I asked.

The years have passed, and now, the snow,
the Leiermann, and grief are one.
I live in comfort. Fortune struck

and fed me with the hand of love,
my scions playing at my feet,
and words of wisdom on my tongue.

But I still see him, slumped before
the television, scratching notes
in algebra – that tragic voice,

which pulled at us, like barking dogs,
whose sorrow, and whose sore complaint
could never tear our worlds apart.

THE PARABLE OF THE PLOUGH

Which of us does not look back?
The years concertina out to show
brief understandings – insights, which
are supremely personal and yours.

You think this is your heritage,
your world, a life, which defies
the darkening hour, or untimely end.
It is experience, and it is truth.

But such imaginings are not your property,
no, no more than the Crown of State.
They are a ghost, a nothing in the mist,
and never will belong to you...

Our lives are tiny rays of light
that cannot stand or rest, but are alive,
a needful touch, a care, a hope
that leaves the future to be famed!

LORRY

On the country road
from Guildford to Chichester,
we were caught behind a lorry
of livestock, heading south.

The autumn sun glinted
on the windscreen, and the trees,
which still maintained their colour:
beeches, chestnuts, oaks.

The lorry gladly bounded
under their great branches,
brushing, blowing, fanning,
the overhanging boughs.

Like flames or ocean waves,
they were possessed of motion.
Happy was that road;
my years, as yet, unpassed.

ETERNITY

I saw eternity, out on the common,
walking his dog, with his sandwiches
that he didn't eat and, with some disquiet,
I hesitated, not knowing how
or whether to greet or nod at him.

"The sky is clear. There was icy weather
last week. Now, I've pressures at work,"
I might have said, but he only
stared at me. My heart was ablaze,
while the taste of death cloyed on my lips.

"If only the sun lasted forever.
If only men's thoughts swam without grief
on a sea of compassion, or if you had spoken,"
he said, "destruction wouldn't have
found you out and menaced your days."

Ashamed, I knew I had forsaken
his art, his friendship, his humorous smile.
I walked alone, in ruined gardens
of vain aspirations and half-ventured wiles,
hoping to hear his voice again.

NOCTURNAL

I can feel this darkness
comes close to me tonight.
No, no, it isn't really dark
but an imperceptibility
clouds the ceiling and the walls.

My lover lies in distant sleep,
as still as the thought that gave
her heart to mine, long before
we came to live, and eat, and breed
together in this building.

The radio, upstairs, is plainly
muffled. And the sombreness of night,
its quiet absences, the awkwardness
of my badly-positioned arm,
the rhythm of my gentle breath,

and the warmth of my body-heat,
underneath the bedding,
make me realise that life,
even in the abstract,
is so very beautiful.

IDEA

Once, someone had an idea.
It was engraved on a pot-shard,
written on parchment,
discussed over supper,
carried on the back during the day,
and swished about in the bottom of tea cups.

People come by, years later,
to destroy the idea,
to up root the forests,
and dance on the pot-shard.
So someone comes along with a mission –
to save an idea.

WORLDLY SILENCE

The stones would love you, if they could,
Probissimus! The song of the icy wind,
in the high trees, would warm your anxious heart
more than garlands heaped on your shoulders
by happy young poets, disciples, and girls.

But the stones do not love. For disorder and
pain, calamity, torture, and vice
surround your darkened sight. And you sit
hoping for quenched thought, ancient kisses
of truth, and answering sighs to visit your grief…

Beyond that – beyond your lamentation –
the voice of a child, born long before
that age you despised, before your ascent
of the sovereign steps of power and art,
heralds your dream and your soul's silence…

SHANTY

Μακάριοι ὁι πτωχοί
Luke 6, 20

A while ago,
in Jakarta, I saw
the shanty towns –
the suburban slums.

I must have been driven
past in a van,
or sat in a train
in a third-class seat.

And I didn't get out
to talk to the poor
that lived under cardboard
or grew up in shacks.

I would have been mobbed
and had quite enough
(poverty – ill-health)
problems to face.

But I witnessed their world,
their solemn despair,
their hearts of ash
and the loaded dice.

In such a place,
you can hardly tell
where the rubbish-tip ends
and the suburb begins.

So I know that we
that pamper ourselves
are not God's people,
are not – the saved!

IN MEMORIAM JENNIFER SWIFT

Like the moon's own face – an Easter moon,
she smiled upon our thorny hearts, our works.
Less than a year ago, she passed
from this to some far-distant
glade, like the college grounds, in peace,
woven with sunlight, former
vanities, and premeditated thought.

Her work was care, concern, the Oxford
loam, which brought forth beetroot, beans,
and brassicas of their various sorts.
Her mind was eager, curious and rich:
unsettled disciplines and redeeming quests.
She lived. She died. So too she spoke.
Those were the many, whom she loved.

SUMMER IN TOWN

On a day like this, the downtown looks like
an architect's model. People roam,
match-stick figures, neither here nor there,
        enlightened and free.

The air is still, a celestial blessing,
and my thoughts – fine-pointed – study the years
that I knew and lost. So many thoughts
        garnered and milled.

Exactness, spare me! Spare me all knowledge!
My heart is brave, but the task is too great
of ever knowing the darkness – the love
        of a world, which is so untrue...

A DARK NIGHT IN GUILDFORD

Lights, from the speeding cars that pass,
from office windows, and the shops,
scatter films of consciousness
on walls, the pavements, passers-by.

Ahead of me, the traffic-lights
burn blood-red, as bloody as
the anger of an empty heart, lost generations,
or of youth unloved, even for its industry.

This is a forsaken place, at once
most prosperous, while yet being stark.
The winter night covers all
my cheerfulness with burgeoning gloom.

Few faces look, or speak to me,
but these are my people: these
three Chinese, a Ukrainian,
two Poles, and two Zimbabweans.

They work in corners, scarcely seen,
admire the world, the lights, the town.
We sit together on the bus,
approaching futures, finding sun.

SPENSER'S OPTICS

Mr Spenser was a physicist.
Working in the mountains
on one invention or another,
he would drive down to teach his class.

Trolleys with tickertape,
cloud chambers, Leyden jars
and Vandergraph generators
buzzed with insight, glinted love.

A pin was set up
on a calibrated board,
lit, projected through the dark
and a well-ground lens.

A focal length of twelve
$1/v = 1/f - 1/u$
$m = v/u$ and the image was
ninety millimetres high.

So, there we were – at fifteen.
We had seen into the eye of life
and ridden on the astral motion
of science and philosophy.

The Almighty had waved at us –
light threading through transparencies
to deposit new ideas
with its even-handedness.

And that is the reason
(Papist though I am)
that I will always honour
the Enlightenment.

TO A CYNIC

The child asks for innocence,
knowing that this will not last,
while the aged learn to forget
everything but sunny thoughts,
and we, between, look towards
accomplishment and shifts of sense.

So, why do you insist,
the world is vain and empty of
cares that echo on the lips,
and say that it will end among
the shy dirge of nothingness,
asteroids and cosmic dust?

THE POET

...Усовершенствуя плоды любимых дум...
Alexander Pushkin

"Is the poet famous?" a voice inquires.
"Oh, no, not very..." "Perhaps,
it was his barbaric education,
his debauchery, or simply the fact
that he kept on going quite mad, but he
is not a famous poet... a wretch, less important,
than, say, a shopkeeper's son..."

What do these voices seek that drive
hard bargains on office phones, or at
webcam meetings? What need have they
for poets – none, perhaps? "A poet, nonetheless!"
But the world wants excitement, scandal and wealth,
in which, with the favours of idleness and power,
it can sit back at ease, claiming fame...

SILK

Life is like a thread of silk.
You pull one way. It pulls the other.
You twiddle it round in an endless loop,
always chasing the end,
but you do not realise the silk is the life,
and you think, "Isn't there something else?"

The thread wears thin, and you play gingerly,
wondering where the adventure will lead.
The silk has a smooth, effortless touch.
You hardly know it is there.
Then, one day, quite by chance, it breaks –
and you have severed your life, your silk.

NO ENVY

I saw you, today, with a beautiful woman,
Probissimus, a girl more beautiful
than the ones that usually sing in church.

She trod gently, and nodded her head in the sun,
unconsciously fanning herself with pride,
while drunks argued and traffic sat in a jam.

And, straight away, I knew that no envy
for such a pearl, for such a destiny,
would ever whisper or rage in me,

that I was happier than you could be,
that the boys on their skate-boards, their dissonant laughs,
their clamour, your hurt and her eyes were your world,

while the leaves on the trees would bleed for me
drops of true love, its smiles and tears,
that, in the heat of the day, I'm busy with work.

WORKING CLASS HEROES

For Nigel

As my fancy-piece would say,
when I used to visit her –
two floors up, supper, smiles – "You're
a working class intellectual!"
It often makes me think
there are different types of these heroes:

like the boy, who was boarder,
schooled, absorbed the arts, but voted Left,
and, unlike his schoolmates, spent his life
in menial jobs, but never grieved
or was daunted by his poverty,
got on with it – enjoyed being free;

or the coarse and blousy girl,
in tatty denim – high-heeled shoes –
who stood in the Proms queue, and maintained,
"I've left 'em all at Knebworth. I've
told 'em, I'm comin' 'ere this ye'r 'cause
I wan' ta dig SHOSTAKOVICH!"

THE LAND

England, the grey covering of the sky,
the empty streets, unsocial sounds,
your half-dismantled tongue,
which isn't spoken so well these days –

all this is much better than
most places I have found on earth:
the innocent fauna of your woods,
a growing season of some months,

and the cattle that break up the views,
food for the table, friends of wealth.

THE HOTEL

On paye au mois...
Guillaume Apollinaire

The world we live in is like a hotel,
although it is not particularly high-class.
Your room may have a view, a drinks' closet,
or, otherwise, your neighbours may be noisy.
If you are lucky, breakfast will be served!
Your business there should be arduous, but,
if things go really well, it'll be a holiday!
Don't spend too much time watching TV!
Get out, look around the town, and see the sights!
Such fine accommodation should be valued.
Keep clean, shower every day, and use the laundry.
Don't over spend! Everyone must pay their bill!
Remember to put things straight and tidy up,
before you pack your bags, check out, and leave...

TO THE RULING CLASS

You are greedy for stupidity.
The child that asks for bread or wisdom
is ruined by your eagerness
to gratify desires.

You think your modern world
more enlightened than Victoriana,
but you cannot see yourselves
lit by learning or historicism.

No honest soul can be believed,
when claiming study and temperance
would rectify our ends,
but they are ridiculed and shunned.

You have the latest thing.
You have it near at hand.
But your vision is only that
that a snail would scarcely boast.

"Sell the nation. Sell every scrap
of education, honesty,
industry and love," is the empty clamour
of your putrid mouths.

FROST ON PAULINE'S ROOF

A daub of glistening, chilly frost
tarnishes my neighbour's roof, today,
just as on any other winter day,
and stands, ill omen, and yet as nothing
more than painted decoration.

Our children are sheltered by these roofs,
their turbulent, antipathetic cries
pounding the walls – their plangent
mockery in our gardens, on fine days:
a simple life, and yet such energy.

The suburbs glow, bright in the sun,
like the rock in Scythia, where Prometheus
was bound in iron – frost, in the early hours –
the torrid day his punishment – just as the lives
of those we know are grafted to these streets.

But we enjoy his gift of fire – fire
for cooking, fire for warmth, and fire
for our hearts, which burn – sometimes in a rage
of post-imperial emptiness, and sometimes glinting
in this, our urban focus of the world.

OWL

...a most melancholy cry...
Edward Thomas

The owl cannot put words to
his joy, his anger, or disquiet,
but skulks, shrieking in the night.

That night, my wife lay very ill,
my friend's wife was dying, and
the broad sea of suffering was mine.

If you asked me the question, "How
can God be all good and all powerful
when there is evil in the world?" I would say

that there must be some impediment,
some gross disunion that lives between
the work of art and its forming hand.

No praise, no hammering, no plea
to end my woes, can mend my loss,
for pain and meaning are as one.

The owl started in the early hours,
and in its dissonance, its disrespect,
life and entreaty brought me hope.

O, STARS

Little lamps on the sea of night,
angels tutoring humble souls,
divided from the earth, you fly
through centuries of hollowness.

A patch of ink, a smear of light,
your greeting is my heart, my bliss,
a word of consolation, or reproach,
water on dryness, a flood on pride.

Give me your unperturbed respect,
your high tranquillity, your grace,
and be above my dreams, my death,
immortal guardians of mortal loss.

THE BARREL

For Edith

Bruce Campilli died at sea. No,
not in action, although the war was on
and he was in the navy. In training,
he fell down a hatch and broke his neck.

He had been my father's only friend
at school. The two of them wrote essays
mocking staff. My father, grieved by the death,
though trained for Burma, saw Italy and Graz.

When Campilli's ship was scrapped,
my father bought an ornament – a barrel
made of its wood, "H.M.S. – the name, the date –"
It sat about on shelves – the mantelpiece.

In the chaos of my infancy – disputes
and turbulence – the barrel came
to have the toothmarks of a two-year-old,
my shame and awkwardness.

It must have been the end for him. The son,
who turned against him, and a wife,
who argued quite unreasonably – all this
flared up in anger – dreams of blood.

But then we flourished, loved again,
beat toothmarks, craziness and pain,
while those, who rested on their dignity,
could never dare to live.

MODERNITY

The girl at the bus-stop
drops her h's, like Sappho.
She seems to have
the same inclinations too.

But her words are not gracious,
nor is her manner reserved,
and she does not honour
reverence and charm.

She swears down her mobile,
hops on the bus –
lovely, desired,
but travelled and free.

REDRESS!

O, Simplicita, you knew nothing
of history, and never took
your part in it. Tyrants rose
and fell; the seas swelled;
men were torn apart in battle,
but your moment never spoke or told.
No envy was yours, but, also, no
care for those that fell, for famines
or nations of prisoners – locked away
to make a ruling class look pure.

But an hour is coming soon,
when you too will be amazed!
Beyond the stars, beyond torture
and death, an immensity of
happy faces will come to celebrate
a freedom, innocent but wild!
They'll laugh, and they'll show
how wrong you were to hide your eye,
to stop your ear and proclaim
that bread and comfort sated you…

SEA VIEWS

I tilt my head in solemn silence,
for that is what she needs –
my salty-sweet lover of the foam.

Sometimes, a storm comes in.
We rage and curse each other,
forgetful of our cordiality.

Then, black night:
the wilderness enrobed
in ignorance and starry charms...

Between it all, I think
into myself, and out again –
oh, the buxom sea!

I sit by a window, which
wafts the smell of bladder-wrack
and laughter on the beach.

WINTER

Winter, my friend, why are you
scratching at the door? Why
are you scampering over
the empty fields and leafless lanes?

Why does the heart no longer enjoy
sunny, early morning walks
along the verge of a country stream,
or bask in the afternoon heat, today?

Why doesn't love spread among
the ritual ease of summer nights,
when voices merge with fleeting shadows,
and make their oaths of loyalty?

But now, people congregate
away from sight, in curtained rooms
or in the dark. Car headlights find us
but hide those steering at the wheel.

Dark deeds, dark thoughts, cold
forebodings, menace our hours,
but those, who have comfort,
company and lodgings rejoice.

For, though your frigid look
is senseless and also cruel
to those that are feeble or frail,
your gibes do not dispirit me.

Your smile is mocking –
your wit sarcastic.
You laugh at bitter irony.
Your eye reveals your secret joys.

I will embrace you, and will claim
you as my own, dear lover,
an introvert, though thoughtful friend –
true justice and true despair!

THE MACHINES

The machines that worked for us
were noisy. – They taught us
their music, wrenched us away
from a sweetheart's kiss, her sighs,
or the child that pleaded for our company.

Under the reach of their iron hand,
we learnt a new intent, a rivalry
of energy, power and ambition.
Their wheels turned for us, but, while
our mouths were full, our tongues were mute.

Don't envy us! Despite our luxuries,
we were a mechanical and doomed
generation, that knew no beauty,
no hunger for humanity!
We were fed, and led, by machines!

THE CYCLISTS

For Tim and Jennifer

We saw them on their bicycles
in Oxford, Cambridge, Islington and Bow
with their toddlers on the back,
on little tandems, twos and threes,
the other kids ahead, reflective belts,
and helmeted. They shopped

fair-trade, ate organic, took the kids
to swimming, judo, basket-ball
and weekend music groups, and they
were a professional class that voted Blair,
but then were horrified at the war.
Some went to church – the mosque.

I think about their work today, for they
fought with chains, valves and pumps,
and twelve pound bags of wholemeal rice,
took holidays, where the kids spoke French,
slaved and cared for future sense. And I pray,
"May everything be all right!"

THE RETURN

...ἐπιστήμη ἡ ἀνδρεία ἐστίν...
The Laches

i

It wasn't exactly a running brook,
but was more like a drainage ditch,
alongside the village road, where Eloise
would stand and stare, in those days.

Supper was graced with the easy talk
of Plato, civil liberties, and the works
of art that spotted various centuries,
and then, of course, there was school.

In that little brook, that drainage ditch,
leaves would saunter on the streams
of autumn gales, light spring rains,
and unexpected summer showers.

Eloise was reared in that world,
like the seed of the fir-cone, or the swift
that flies from his nest in the Norman spire,
lofty and high, enquiring abroad.

ii

Returning from study,
quadrangles and gowns,
Eloise was now
grown and formed,
and she saw old Jack Emas
hunched on his gate,
enjoying that August
evening's shade.

"I'm sorry to hear, your old man
has passed away," he said, staring straight
into her space. "His business, of course,
wasn't my affair. But I respected his type,
the kind of person he was. And
I don't think I'll hear much of his sort again,
on Friday nights – his sensible talk,
among the rest of us, in the Public Bar..."

Eloise was touched,
but well-composed,
thought well of the man,
who had always stood
hunched at his gate,
a pillar of truth,
a solitary token
of human thought.

"It really is terribly nice of you
to speak of my late father like that.
He had a peaceful death, and his life
was fulfilling and long. I couldn't have wished
for a better light to guide my early years.
I knew him as well as I know myself.
So, although you might think it strange,
I feel no loss at his subsequent parting."

iii

It was the age of the car, the siren and plane,
and Eloise had a fretful life.
People rocked, and people were blue.
There was noise and profanity everywhere.

It was also the age of conspicuous wealth,
and sayings like, "When the going gets tough,
the tough get going," and, "On your bike!"
Existence became begrudging and mean.

The house on the village street was sold,
and Eloise then reached that age,
when youth no longer sports easily
and fortune is felt to be slipping by.

Janette, her friend, said, "Dear Eloise,
I see life scolds and chastises you.
Come, party with those that can bring you cheer!
We'll make you daring, worldly and free!"

iv

Six of them went out to dance,
    at a nightclub,
    beside the docks.
The party was blithe, cheerful and bright.
    The bar was full
    and thundered with sound.

A stranger's eye was on Eloise,
    but then, in the heat
    of a jealous dispute,
a fight broke out, and poor Eloise
    lost her handbag
    and was pushed to the ground.

Recriminations and scuffles ensued,
    but by the time
    the police were called,
and took a statement from Eloise,
    the party-goers
    had disappeared.

A flat-featured man came up to her,
    gave her a smile
    and extended a hand.
"There's a restaurant, not far," he said to her.
    "I'll take you there.
    You need to relax!"

v

"The *coq au vin*'s not bad! Please,
take a seat. I saw it all
with my own eyes! They wanted your bag!
Do you know that Micky lad?
Clearly, you were the victim of
a very clever confidence trick!"

The waiter came. They ordered drinks.
The night was dyed in grievous tints.
Then that man spoke again,

"My flat's only in Belsize Park.
I'll order a taxi to take you there.
Those villains are really after you!
They'll have you again. And you
really should be tucked up in bed!
You know, you'd be safer there!"

"Okay. But first, I must be excused,"
said Eloise, and slipped out the back.
She left him there, and went for help.

vi

Love is the only creature I know
that brings me brightness and ease.
And, some months later, that creature found
Eloise, on the train to Potters Bar.

The name of this species of love, or *amour*,
was "Steve". He was smart and curious.
He wooed his girl with passion and fun,
a divine messenger, serving her heart.

They went on buses to abbeys and shows,
and sat in cafés in Museum Street,
discussing all the things they had seen,
and spent nights together, exploring touch.

"Darling Eloise," said Steve, one day,
"please, marry me and start a tribe
of little Eloises and Steves!
We'll build a house of pleasantness."

"I cannot say, "yes," to you, today,"
answered Eloise, a little curt.
"For, firstly, I must go and see
the village that was once my home…"

vii

"There's nothing left, here, for me,"
          thought Eloise,
looking around her old village streets,
          "no faces I know,
          or shops I used,
and the autumn sky is angry and grey!"

She paced about, in a desultory mood,
       flitting and flying
her corners and turns, until she came
       to the cottage, where
       a wizen Jack Emas
still managed to stand and lean on his gate...

"Sir!" she said. "Please, old Jack,
       speak to me!
Tell me, where I can find my love,
       where the faces I knew,
       the laughter and talk
of those simple years can be found?

Tell me, where the sky meets the earth,
       where pleasant debate
still lives and still breeds,
       and pain and distress
       are left behind,
where the healing whisper of truth has its nest?"

"Listen to the wind!" the old man said,
       bent and blind,
hunched over his gate. "Listen,
       like rabbits,
       foxes and hares!
Listen to your heart bleed for time!"

Eloise then bolted, and fled, aghast,
       down to the trees
by the drainage ditch, and said to herself,
       "The leaves float
       in this ugly ditch,
as my life should float on earthly lips!"

THE SONG OF THE DINOSAURS

Dr Zerkalo lived in a town house,
up on the hill, alongside the park,
among those that worked in Whitehall, or earned
their livings in the City, in finance or stocks.

But, down below, in the haphazard streets,
in a tiny flat, at the top of a house,
surrounded by noises from lorries and shops,
sat Eustace, alone: a poet of dreams.

His room was untidy. There was nothing to eat.
The lighting was dim. There lay on the floor
piles of books, newspapers, and clothes,
worn out records, and half-written verse.

The weather was clear. No telephone stood,
ready to ring, by the wall, in the flat.
The evening looked long, and dusk came too soon,
so Eustace decided to go up to the park.

He had known the Zerkalos, for one or two years.
Their daughter was fine, and talked about books.
And, walking beside the headlights and cars,
he decided to call, in search of a snack.

Mrs Zerkalo answered. Red hair and blue eyes
gleamed in the porch-light, as she smiled, and then
welcomed him in, into light, into warmth,
into the kitchen, which steamed and smelt good.

"Is Dr Zerkalo here?" Eustace began,
awkward and tugging the hem of his coat.
"And Anna? Oh, no! She must be away?
Her studies are good? I'm sure she does well!"

"All fine!" Mrs Zerkalo sang, with a look
of startled surprise, of interest, and love.
"Would you like to stay, Eustace, for tea?
I've something prepared, a weekend feast."

Eustace grinned, and his words also sang,
as he assented, and thanked her kindness, her thought.
"I'd be delighted! I've hardly eaten for days!
If you don't mind me saying, that's splendid of you!"

"Vlad's next door. He's reading a book.
Go and tell him you're here. He'd like to talk.
We have soup and fish and plenty of bread.
Go through! He might even give you a drink!"

Eustace took her advice, and went through the door
and across the hall, to the lounge, where, old
and retired, Dr Zerkalo sat, engrossed in a book.
"Ah, Eustace!" he huffed, and rose to his feet.

Flapping his arms, he offered a chair. "How are you,
young man? Are you well? Are you writing?
What books have you read? I'm sorry, I've nothing
to offer you here. But Hilda is cooking, so stay!"

The two of them talked, and sat, and talked
about science and art, and all manner of things.
Between language and books, and manners and race,
and atoms and radar, and planets and stars,

they took their course, and patched up old ends,
made substance of air, and reason of words,
in the darkness of evening, which was clear and cold,
before Dr Zerkalo said, "A vodka, perhaps?"

He had only just opened the mahogany door
of the drinks' cabinet, and pulled out
the bottle, whose simple label was worn,
when Mrs Zerkalo called them to eat.

"This is genuine Russian vodka,"
he said, with a smile, gripping the neck
with his powerful hand, as he showed Eustace
back through to the kitchen, to the family table.

Spread before Eustace, were bowls and plates,
bread, biscuits, cheese and soup,
which all lay ready. Light gilded the spoons,
which glowed with invitations of health.

They sat down to borsch, a beetroot soup,
which was made from produce grown in the garden,
and bread that was bought in a specialist shop,
which only sold loaves to the rich and discerning.

"Anna says you play the violin, Eustace,"
Mrs Zerkalo said, at the end of the soup.
"What sort of things do you play?
Do you listen to music much in your flat?"

"I play a few tunes, but not very well.
I play Schumann, Handel, Beethoven and Brahms.
But I listen to records, as much as I can,
especially the English and Russian greats.

The Post-Wagnerians were the love of my life,
until I returned to Beethoven again.
And now I think I'm changing my taste,
to that of the Classical-Romantic world.

Beethoven's genius towers, sublime!
There's pure music in his every note!
And, even if it's unnerving and crazed,
his imagination surpasses all.

Of course, he wasn't exactly mad,
but was easily angered, and lost many friends.
His place is unique in Western art,
though sadly deaf, a giant of sound!"

As if to speak, Dr Zerkalo buckled his lips,
but stretched out his arm to take some bread,
which he placed beside him, and broke off a piece,
and rubbed his fingers, before he spoke,

"You see, Beethoven had a different brain!
His temporal lobes were greatly enlarged,
and this is the part which governs our sense
of hearing, and this aided his art.

So, all the others can't compare,
to this creature, who, in many ways,
had a brain, as reptiles do, extended where
the mind of hearing and music is."

Though taken aback, Eustace needed to speak,
to answer this man, who probed deeper than him.
"Yes, there must be some truth in that!
Birds are related to reptiles, and known for song!"

But all he received, by way of reply,
was a knowing nod, a hint of a smile,
and the knowledge that he'd learnt something,
once more, before Mrs Zerkalo said,

"Fish pie everyone? Today's my treat!
There's nothing else with it. It's all in the one.
I bought the fish, this morning, at Tom's.
The fishmonger's girl said they might close!"

Dr Zerkalo opened the vodka, and they
gossiped and dined, for over an hour,
setting things right, over biscuits and cheese,
before Mrs Zerkalo made another suggestion,

"Eustace, Vlad has his old violin, upstairs.
Would you like to play a duet with me?
I play the piano. I'm a little bit rusty."
"Certainly!" Eustace barked, keen with drink.

Vlad went to get his instrument,
which was somewhat flat, and the bow
was too light for Eustace, who then retuned,
put the shoulder-rest on, and practised a bit.

Mrs Zerkalo reached for one of her scores,
while her husband set up the music stand.
"*Die Frülings Sonate*?" she asked. "Of course!
How did you guess?" Eustace replied.

Gingerly, keenly, they played through the score
of the first movement, and achieved their aim
of playing together, but, exhausted and drunk,
Eustace conceded, "We're not very good!"

"Why don't you play the Russian songs,
Hilda, my love?" mumbled Vlad.
"Yes, dear! But don't you think we'll need
a little more vodka, if we do?"

Agreeing, she dug out a tatty volume,
as Vlad poured the vodka. The title page said,
"*Popular Russian Songs*", in Cyrillic script, and,
pencilled throughout, were the English words.

Stooping to read, over Hilda's shoulder,
Eustace played along, and they sang,
Katyusha, Dark Eyes, Slim Rowan Tree,
and three or four others, between rounds of drink.

By the end of the evening, they both played
so badly, that it was foolery.
But they all had such fun, that Eustace left
lighter in heart, fulfilled, and free.

He walked in the quiet, morning streets,
back to his flat, took off his shoes,
lay down, beside his unfolded clothes,
on the bed, and went directly to sleep.

He awoke to the sound of falling trees,
and a tropical heat made him sweat.
A sound, so full and beautiful,
rang in his ears, and made his heart pound.

It was the sound of singing dinosaurs:
a chorus more thrilling than anything heard
in concert halls, or upper-class salons,
the sound of visceral harmony.

The air was rich, and animal smells
floated across the Jurassic woods,
and sopranos, tenors, bases, and altos
sang antiphonal cries of joy and distress.

Such love of sound, such love of the voice,
had never greeted his ears before.
It was primitive, and liberated,
enveloping him in passion and fear.

Some creatures happily tore down trees,
were benign, and entirely innocent,
while others raged, and bellowed, with blood
in their mouths, left from gory feasts.

But there was no morality, no shame,
self-conscious doubt, scruple or qualm,
among their thoughts, but only the art
of music adorned their happy days.

He wanted to sing with the dinosaurs,
and started to whine, to whinny, to howl,
but, sensing that he was being pursued,
he began to run, and ran, and ran.

At the extremity of delight and dread,
he heard an animal gaining on him. Just as
he felt himself about to be gorged, lightning
struck him, and blew him to bits...

When Eustace awoke the second time,
it was to the sound of a winter storm.
He sat up in bed, and turned on the light,
and said, "*That* was the song of the dinosaurs!

That's the reason the dinosaurs died,
were driven from earth, and became extinct,
because they all had such musical minds,
which engaged them in a love of song!

So they lost the will to live, being full
of beauty, freedom, and happiness!"
Our poet then went to write his poem
to explain the gift of the dinosaur race.

BY THE RIVER GRETA

Just as a mountain stream races
after rain, or an unbroken horse shies,
when on the busy road, so,
likewise, my youth was fey, swollen
with energy – unleashed before the hare!

The deep foliage of the woods, up
above the River Greta, is
silent and unbowed. Within
that early turmoil, my passionate unease,
were simplicities as knowing.

No one can ever find their birth,
climb to a point, which sees beyond
the substance of their world, those small
and curious inconveniences,
which keep them living, keep them strong.

And yet, like anyone, who trod the path
of thoughtfulness, who breathes and reads,
I have discovered answers in
the leaf's elegance, or thunder of the flood,
which satisfy my longing.

No time, no emptiness, is mine.
No feast returns me to my innocence.
The light is like a blessing from on high,
but labours weary me, and worries scatter all
I ever held as dear, in patchy heaps.

The fairy foxglove, in the wood, does not
entirely conceal itself, but shows
a touch of colour, a spot of tenderness,
and, like the many revelations of the heart,
nature's underside will be exposed.

This age may fail, or it may promise more,
but each of us must dance in battle with
untidy sloth, violent disarray, and pains
that muddy thought, and yet I still compel
the hand of fate with a daring calm.

In stillness, or in peaceable debate,
which centres on the origin of years,
the vision of my future is begun. So I
urge deliberation on myself – the track
that joins and rejoins human gentleness.

Yes, my age was noisy, and a riot
of ugly sentiment abounds,
vying for an ear, and for a place
among the ranks of those sanctified
heroes of popular demand.

But I am glad, these voices do not speak
to my inner ear, or make me deviate
my course, like sirens leading mariners
towards the rocks, although there have been times,
when I, also, considered myself theirs.

The world of gossip and of influence,
therefore, does not appeal to me. Its
hollow ring is treacherous and sly. Although
its name is often "fame", I dare say,
"fame" is not the study honoured there.

What fear walks before me? Perhaps, it is
to be thrown, like so many, to the wind,
dispersed into a nothingness
of needful displeasure, and
lost to any semblance of a mind?

But love lies naked, ready to be grasped.
It is a warmth of habitual speech,
a sympathy of ear and touch,
an eye that neither sleeps, nor burns in rage,
and charity towards a heart's design...

But love is what I always knew.
Even in my rustic solitude,
it cried among the bushes and the ferns,
proclaiming a companionable response
of sky, and river, and of humble lips...

Now, too, I often stand alone,
removed from the chaos of the herd,
but separated not by place or work,
but rather mood and learning – even thought,
which is related to philosophy...

So, as I fade, not knowing whether these
words I save are due to perish too,
I defy the vehemence of the crowd.
While resting in the shade of trees and books,
I also know the greater part is mine!

ACKNOWLEDGEMENTS

Working Class Heroes published in ACUMEN 2009
Spenser's Optics published in THE SHOP 2010
The Surrey Hills published in ACUMEN 2011

FOREIGN LANGUAGE HEADERS AND QUOTES

Fly Page, Laozi, "What's so empty in the ancient saying,
"Bowed down and then preserved"?
Truly with that you can last out and achieve your end."

En Locatif, French, "In the Locative", a grammatical case
describing a point of place or time.

Der Leiermann, "The hurdy-gurdy man",
the last song in Schubert's cycle *Die Winterreise.*

Luke 6, 20, "Blessed are the poor…"

Alexander Pushkin, "…Perfecting the fruits of your favourite thoughts…"

Guillaume Apollinaire, "One pays monthly…"

Plato, *The Laches,* "…knowledge is courage…"

INDEX